The Autoworker's Guide to Lump Sum Pensions

Richard Paul, CFP®

& Steven Paul, CFP®

This publication contains the opinions and ideas of its authors. The strategies outlined in this book may not be suitable for every individual and are not guaranteed or warranted to produce any particular results. Presentation of performance data herein does not imply that similar results will be achieved in the future. Any such data are provided merely for illustrative and discussion purposes, rather than focusing on the time periods used or the results derived. The reader should focus instead on the underlying principles. This book is sold with the understanding that neither publisher nor author, through this book, is engaging in rendering legal, tax, investment, insurance, financial, accounting or other professional advice or services. If the reader requires such advice or services, a competent professional should be consulted. Relevant laws vary from state to state.

No warranty is made with respect to the accuracy or the completeness of the information contained herein, and both the author and the publisher specifically disclaim any responsibility for any liability, loss, or risk, personal or otherwise, that is incurred as a consequence, directly or indirectly, of the use and application of any of the contents of this book. The ideas expressed are not meant to be taken as advice that you can act upon. You should find an individual advisor that you trust to implement these ideas after determining if they are appropriate and suitable for your unique situation. Insurance Products and Annuities are guaranteed by the insurance companies themselves. The safety of these accounts is dependent on the claims-paying ability of the issuing insurance companies.

Certified Financial Planner Board of Standards Inc. owns the certification marks CFP®, CERTIFIED FINANCIAL PLANNER™ and CFP® (with flame design) in the U.S., which it awards to individuals who successfully complete CFP Board's initial and ongoing certification requirements.

Richard W. Paul & Associates, LLC is an SEC Registered Investment Advisory firm. Midwest Financial Consultants, Inc is an Insurances Services firm. Investment Advisory Services offered through Richard W. Paul & Associates, LLC.

Copyright © 2019 Richard Paul & Steven Paul

All rights reserved.

ISBN: 9781088885635

TABLE OF CONTENTS

1	The million-dollar question	Pg 1
2	Why is my company offering me a lump sum?	Pg 4
3	What are my options?	Pg 15
4	What are the fundamental factors to making this decision?	Pg 31
5	How do I incorporate my 401(k) with my pension lump sum?	Pg 38
6	What are the key planning opportunities to consider?	Pg 46
7	What are the things not to do?	Pg 57
8	How can I find a financial advisor to help with all of this?	Pg 62
9	When should I file for social security?	Pg 71
10	How do annuities work?	Pg 76
	Conclusion	Pg 84

CHAPTER 1

THE MILLION-DOLLAR QUESTION

> *"Before everything else, getting ready is the secret of success."*
>
> – Henry Ford

Have you ever heard the phrase "the sixty-four-thousand-dollar question" before? It dates all the way back to the 1940s and was the question asked at the climax of the British radio quiz show *Take it or Leave it*. This question was later popularized in the United States during the 1950s on the game show *The $64,000 Question*. If you were to use this phrase today when talking to your kids or grandkids, they might look at you a bit funny, as they're likely more familiar with the 1999 version of the phrase—"the million-dollar question"—from *Who Wants to Be a Millionaire?*

We all remember this show: the unique set, the stage lighting, the intense sound effects, and of course, the dramatic, drawn-out pauses Regis Philbin would make after asking, *"Is that your final answer?"*

The contestant would have the choice to walk away with money in hand or continue risking it as they advanced in the game. Rarely, the contestant would make it to the million-dollar question, and if they got the question wrong, they would fall all the way back down to $32,000; but if they got it right, they walked away with a life-changing sum of money.

As an autoworker, you may be faced with a similar million-dollar decision at retirement. If it's not quite a million dollars, it's still likely a significant sum of money that could impact your family for generations to come. Now, you won't have the award-winning gameshow host or the dramatic lighting as you face this decision, but for some who haven't thought through their plan, it can certainly feel that way.

To take it a step further, when planning out your retirement, you will most likely be faced with not only one million-dollar question, but several:

1. Do I take the lifetime pension or the lump sum?
2. If I take the lump sum, how can I keep it protected from market volatility while still generating consistent income?
3. What do I do with my 401(k) when I retire?
4. When do I take my social security?
5. How do I find a trusted advisor to help with all of this?

These are some of the most crucial financial decisions you'll face in your lifetime, and you want to make sure you get them right. This book will primarily focus on the decision to take your pension in the form of monthly payments—as it was originally promised to you when your employment began—or as a lump sum one-time payment and roll it over into an Individual Retirement Account (IRA). We'll then discuss how you can incorporate this along with your other investments and social security into your overall income plan.

It is important to understand you are not alone in this decision. This book was written to help you better understand the pros and cons of the choices you have. The decision of taking your lump sum or not is a decision that many people have had to make, and quite frankly, one that many people are intimidated by.

Our hope is that as you read through this book, your peace of mind increases, and your anxiety diminishes. The goal of this book is not to sway you in one direction or the other, it's to use our experience in the industry to help alleviate some of the stress this decision may cause you. We have designed this guide to provide you with the basics you'll need to help in your decision making.

Just like in *Who Wants to Be a Millionaire*, it's a rarity for someone to make it to the end to answer the million-dollar question, and you've done just that.

Congrats! If you're reading this book, you've made it through a long career in the auto industry and are facing this life-changing decision. **It's a good thing**, but approach it cautiously, carefully evaluate your options, and most importantly, take a deep breath.

CHAPTER 2

WHY IS MY COMPANY OFFERING ME A LUMP SUM?

"The trouble with most people is that they think with their hopes or fears or wishes rather than with their minds."

– Will Durant

The concept of guaranteed lifetime income dates as far back as Ancient Rome, when veterans of the Imperial Roman Army were given a permanent revenue source in exchange for their service. Suffice to say, the pension concept has evolved quite substantially since that time. The first U.S. company to offer the private pensions that autoworkers are familiar with today was American Express in 1875.

Pensions were of tremendous benefit to retirees and were a critical element that many retirees depended on for a successful retirement. But the pension obligations started to grow so large they became burdensome for companies to sustain, so much so that many companies found they'd overcommitted themselves and were not able to fulfil the promises they'd made to their employees. Many retirees learned the hard way that there wasn't much of a back-up plan in place for them if their company were to fail.

Many in the auto industry might be familiar with Studebaker, the car manufacturer out of South Bend, Indiana. In 1963, Studebaker terminated its pension plan, causing four thousand autoworkers to lose some or all of their pension benefits.

Over the next decade, more and more plans were failing, and finally, in 1974, **ERISA** created the Pension Benefit Guaranty Corporation (**PBGC**). The PBGC would provide a back-up plan to give retirees greater assurance that their pensions would last for their lifetime. We will discuss the PBGC in more detail in the next chapter.

In 1978, Congress enacted the Revenue Act, which created the defined contribution structure of saving for retirement. Your 401(k) is an example of this. In the 1980s, these defined contribution plans started to gain popularity as companies began shifting away from the defined benefit pension plans and more to the defined contribution system of saving for retirement. This shifted the burden of saving and investing from the company to the employee.

As an autoworker, you could have the best of both worlds, as you might have both a defined benefit pension and a 401(k) savings plan!

The Lump Sum Pension

Let's discuss why companies like Ford, General Motors and Fiat-Chrysler give you the option to take a lump sum payment upon retirement, instead of beginning a monthly pension payment.

For simplicity, let's say you started working at your company at age thirty, and their pension plan says that if you work until age sixty-five, the company will pay you $5,000 a month for the rest of your life. It also says you have the option to take a reduced benefit, in which they will pay you and your spouse that money for the rest of your lives, even if you were to pass away first.

Because they have made that promise, you are now a creditor of the company. These lifetime payments represent a future liability on the books that only goes away once you (and possibly your spouse) pass away. As public companies, these future pension liabilities are reflected as a debt item on their balance sheet. Multiply that by thousands upon thousands of retirees, and those future pension liabilities become an outrageous number.

Ford, General Motors and Fiat-Chrysler must predict, for all the workers they have on the books, approximately how long each of them is likely to live and how much the company can earn on money set aside until then. Then they fund the plan based on these calculations. The companies also need to show the results of that analysis, their future pension liabilities, as a debt on the company balance sheet.

But why are they offering a present-day lump sum in exchange for my pension?

Let's think of it from your company's perspective. One million dollars is nothing to them. They'd rather not have that future liability sitting there on their balance sheet for the next two to three decades (or possibly longer!). They'd much rather write you a check, kiss you out the door, and be off the hook, rather than deal with an increasing future financial obligation they're unable to control.

Companies of this size like control and predictability. It's important to bear in mind that the obligation to pay you gets larger or smaller as it remains on the company balance sheet based on three primary factors that are out of their control:

#1: Discount Rate

The first factor that can make the anticipated obligation larger or smaller is the current interest rate, or as actuaries call it, the discount rate. The higher the interest rate, the easier it is to make money on your money. For example, say the current rate drops from four percent to three percent—a lower rate would cause an increase in pension expense, and result in an increase in the future liability.

The General Agreement on Tariffs and Trade Rate (GATT Rate) is the 30-year Treasury Bond interest rate and is often used as a benchmark for calculations of lump sum distribution from defined benefit plans. The graph on the following page illustrates how this rate trended down from 1991 to 2018, with 2018 reversing the trend. This was the first time we saw an annual increase since 1990!

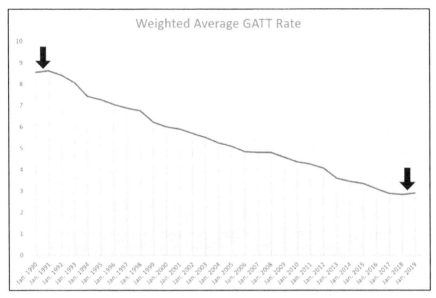

Data Source: IRS.gov[1]

This is very significant. You will see your lump sum value decline when this rate increases. The almost two-decade decreasing trend appears to have bottomed out, and possibly reversed. Let's say, hypothetically, your lump sum pension is valued at $1 million; there is a very real possibility that it will be a six-figure pension compared to a seven-figure pension if you wait a few years to retire <u>and</u> this rate continues to increase. Knowing this, many retirees who are leaning toward taking the lump sum may opt to retire sooner than anticipated, so they don't see a negative adjustment to their lump sum value.

Think of it as a seesaw. One side of the seesaw is the future liability of the company offering the pension, the other side of the seesaw is interest rates. When rates go down, this pushes the liability up. When rates go up, the liability goes down. Again, this is very important, because we are now in what will likely be an extended rising interest rate environment, considering the all-time interest rate lows we have seen since the 2008 recession. **Each time interest rates go up, your pension lump sum value goes down.**

#2: Life Expectancy

The next factor that can come into play and affect the obligation is life expectancy. This is the easiest to understand, as the longer you live, the longer they have to pay. And people are living longer than ever. In 1980, your company could reasonably expect a seventy-year-old male retiree to live just another 11.9 years. Some would live longer, some would pass away sooner, but with the law of large numbers on their side, this would be an accurate number. Retirees who lived into their mid-eighties and nineties would be offset by those who passed away in their seventies.

Fast forward to today, and the average life expectancy for a seventy-year-old male is reaching well into the mid-eighties. When the pension plan was instituted, the company anticipated a certain amount that they would have to pay out, based on life expectancy in retirement. Now, people are living much longer, and because they're living longer, the company will be obligated to pay out much more than they originally planned. As medical technology continues to advance and people are living healthier lifestyles, this obviously adds uncertainty.

On the following page, a study from PGIM illustrates how increases in longevity impact pension liabilities.[2] Each time mortality tables are released, the increases in longevity result in a corresponding increase to the liabilities of these pension plans.

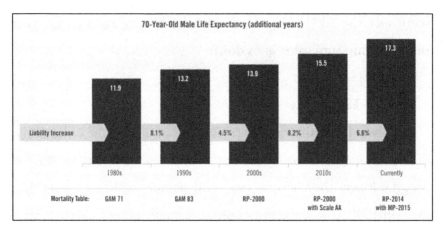

As you can see, each time there has been an increase in life expectancy on the mortality tables, the liability increases have ranged from 4.5 percent to 8.2 percent. As longevity increases, so do the pension liabilities, as the company will have to pay out for a longer period of time.

But isn't the average life expectancy more like seventy-nine for men and eighty-two for women?

Yes, but whenever you see average life expectancy, that will typically be the average life expectancy from birth. When you look at the life expectancy for the age you've reached, you're in a select group of people who have been healthy enough to live as long as you, and the statistical weighting of those who have already passed has been eliminated.

For reference, the chart on the following page shows the average life expectancies for a sixty-five-year-old.[3]

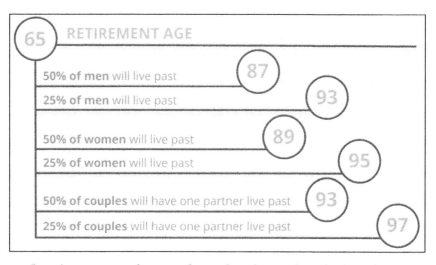

One important takeaway from the above chart is that if you are married and age sixty-five, there is a greater-than-50-percent chance that one of you will live into your early nineties. Therefore, if you are taking some sort of spousal benefit on your pension, you are going to have to take a pay reduction, as the likelihood of paying out for a long time increases dramatically.

#3: Investment Earnings

The third factor that affects whether the company's future pension payment obligations will be larger or smaller is the potential for future investment earnings. Companies don't know with any certainty what they are going to earn on their investments, and that can be an important variable.

To illustrate that, let's assume Ford expects to earn 6.75 percent on their investments over the long-term. With roughly $40 billion in plan assets, if they met their return goal of 6.75 percent, that would increase their plan assets by $2.7 billion. That growth will go a long way toward making up for some of their future obligations. In good years, like 2017, they do not have to fund their investment account as much, because they're earning more on each dollar invested.

On the flip side, if they do not meet return expectations, this means they may need to kick in some extra money to pay their future pension obligations. When you hear that a pension is "underfunded," this simply means they don't have the requisite assets to fund the future liabilities.

Real-World Stats

A study by Pensions & Investments analyzed the SEC filings of a hundred of the largest U.S. corporate-defined benefit plans.[4] Because of interest rate increases throughout 2018, the discount rates of these plans increased by 0.57% to an average of 4.25%, which dropped the aggregate pension liabilities by $117 billion. That shows how increasing rates can have a drastic impact on the future liabilities of the companies, and how when we see positive rate adjustments, you can expect a reduction in your lump sum value.

Although the liabilities lowered due to the discount rate adjustment, much of this benefit was offset due to the poor investment performance of the plan assets. The average return for the hundred companies in 2018 was -3.53% for 2018. Investment return is a key factor and the most difficult to predict for these companies. Many of the past issues with underfunded pensions have been caused by unrealistic investment return targets of 8% to 10%. The average expected return of these hundred companies dropped from 7.94%, in 2011, to a much more reasonable 7%, in 2018.

The Balance Sheet

There's an old joke that Ford and GM are actually just pension companies that are funded by an automobile operation.

Think of that from an investor standpoint. It's certainly not good. Wall Street analysts hate uncertainty and large liabilities. That is why your company is giving you the choice at retirement of taking a lump sum or taking monthly payments.

This is also why many companies are offloading some of their pension liability to annuity companies, like General Motors did in 2012 when they sold over $25 billion in future pensions to Prudential Financial.[5] They'd rather pay an upfront premium and transfer that future liability to a company that specializes in that area. In this case, GM paid a hefty premium by transferring $29 billion to cover roughly $25 billion in pension liabilities.

The bottom line is that these companies are in the business of manufacturing cars, not managing pensions. There are numerous factors in constant motion that affect the size of the pension liability, and they are under a lot of pressure from Wall Street to lessen that uncertainty.

It's not a scam, and they're not out to get you. They would simply rather rid themselves of these enormous future liabilities and get them off the books. Truth be told, they are hoping that as many people as possible elect to take the lump sum payment upon retirement. When that happens, the company makes the lump sum payment, and they get it off their books for good.

The Lump Sum Calculation

One of the major concerns that we hear from retirees facing the lump sum decision is that their company is out to get them. They don't trust the big corporation and feel there's some sort of ulterior motive behind this offer.

In our opinion, that's not the case. One exercise to help retirees understand this is to run a calculation of what the present value of all those future payments would be. This is an exercise you can do yourself by simply searching "Present Value of Future Payments Calculator" in Google and entering in your monthly payments and your life expectancy. For instance, if you plugged in that you would receive $60,000 annually over 25 years (with a 4% interest rate), the calculator would tell you that these future payments have a present-day lump sum value of $937,325.

This helps to illustrate that it's not a trick. It's simply a mathematical calculation done by your company to come up with a fair offer to their employees who were loyal to them over their careers.

CHAPTER 3

WHAT ARE MY OPTIONS?

"I think the mind should deliver new and fresh designs all the time."
- Sergio Marchionne

As you're considering your options, it's important to understand that if you choose the lump sum over the monthly payments, you are shifting the investment risk from the company to yourself. If you take a monthly payout, that risk is on the company. They guarantee your payments, month after month, for the rest of your life. (And there is the federal government's Pension Benefit Guaranty Corporation, which stands behind your company within certain limits in case they were to go bankrupt).

If you decide to take a lump sum payment, you have many potential benefits, but you are now responsible for investing the money (or you need to find a financial advisor you trust to manage the money for you). As we discuss your options in this chapter, we will break them down into the two basic choices you have. But in each instance, there are also numerous other decisions you can make that will affect the payment you receive.

For instance, should you decide to stick with the traditional monthly payment for the rest of your life, there are some additional choices you can make once you've made that initial decision. You can take slightly less each month and have the payments continue throughout your spouse's life, should they live longer. This is a highly personal decision that will vary from couple to couple.

Before getting into the more intricate details, let's spend some time examining the initial critical choice that needs to be made: taking a lump sum for your pension versus leaving things as they are and going ahead with the monthly payout.

Option One: Lump Sum Payment

If you elect to take the lump sum, you are likely proceeding with a rollover to an IRA. You are rolling the money from the pension plan over to a pre-tax IRA, and then you are going to invest the money so that you can plan for the long term and generate income based on your monthly needs. Any withdrawals from this IRA will be subject to income tax (there may be a small portion of the money that is considered after-tax money that you do not need to pay taxes on).

As was mentioned earlier in this book, there are pros and cons to taking the money. You are now responsible for investing the money, which many people would view as a disadvantage, precisely because the risk is being shifted to you—or you along with your team of financial advisors. Once all the money is spent, it's gone.

Others would argue it is an opportunity, depending upon their degree of confidence in their—or your team's—investing expertise.

Another potential disadvantage to consider is if either you or your spouse aren't the best with money, and you tend to spend too much or invest poorly. If that is an appropriate description, you may not want to give yourself access to the pension money through a lump sum payout.

Be honest with yourself; if you are a person with a track record of running up credit card debt or spending excessively, it may make more sense for you not to take the lump sum. If you have jumped in and out of the market at the wrong times, can you expect to treat this money better? Sometimes, it's a matter of being better safe than sorry—the dependable monthly payment may be a better choice than having your entire pension benefit paid all at once just as you start retirement, leaving you with the potential to squander it when you need it most.

The major benefit to taking the lump sum is control. You have the money; you pick how it's invested. This allows you to customize the money to your unique needs.

Keeping it simple, there are two primary ways you can invest your lump sum. You can roll the funds into your IRA and invest in the typical at-risk world of investments—stocks, bonds, ETFs, mutual funds, real estate, etc. —and let the money grow while taking income as needed. We refer to this as "At-Risk" money as it can appreciate and depreciate due to outside factors.

The other world, the guaranteed world, is much safer. This is where you bring in an insurance company to provide either protection against market losses or a guaranteed lifetime income stream. This would be an annuity. The words annuity and pension can almost be used synonymously. In fact, in some languages, there is only one word to describe a stream of income, where in the United States we have two (pensions are income streams guaranteed by employers while annuities are income streams guaranteed by insurance companies). In essence, your pension acts as an annuity, and an annuity can act the same as a pension.

Continuing to attempt to keep it simple, these two basic worlds of investing can provide four primary options to allocate your lump sum, broken down as follows:

	Safe Approach	At-Risk Approach
Safe Approach	100% Safe	Safety Focused with Some Risk
At-Risk Approach	Risk Focused With Some Safety	100% At-Risk

We've said this before, and we'll say it again: there is no single correct choice. Everyone is different; every situation is different.

The first shaded box, the 100% Safe box, is most like your pension. This involves combining various annuity strategies to generate a consistent and reliable income, regardless of market conditions. This can be structured in a variety of ways using immediate annuities and deferred fixed or fixed indexed annuities. In Chapter 10 of the book, we explain the different types of annuities in more detail.

The pro to this strategy is that you can take control of the principal, which means you can still generate a guaranteed income stream, while also having the potential to leave this money to your heirs (depending on how the annuities are structured, this potential may vary). Many people are comfortable with this approach, as they like the comfort of the guaranteed monthly income, which is what they envisioned this money would do for them all along. Others like this approach because they are not confident in the long-term outlook of their company and do not want to fall back on the **PBGC**.

The last shaded box, the 100% At-Risk box, is the complete opposite. This involves taking your pension lump sum and allocating it to the At-Risk world of investing. Now, this doesn't mean taking your lump sum and investing it all in stocks—that would not be recommended unless you had no plans to touch this money and were willing to ride the rollercoaster of the market. This would likely be a balanced allocation of stocks, bonds, and alternatives. The various weightings would primarily depend on your risk tolerance and income needs.

The other two options are both combinations of the At-Risk and Safe worlds of investing. Some people prefer the foundation of their lump sum to be protected from the whims of the market, to generate the income they need to cover their essential expenses regardless of market conditions. Beyond that, they can then invest the remainder for long-term growth. Others prefer a smaller, pension-like income to combine with social security, while having more of the funds geared toward long-term growth and future income.

Again, this is an overly simplistic explanation to help you understand the basic concepts of how you can invest this money. We urge you to meet with a qualified financial professional to help explain these options in more detail and help you figure out what's best for you.

We will issue a word of caution: Be aware how the financial advisor you meet with is licensed. If the financial advisor is only securities licensed, they will be more biased in recommending the At-Risk world of investing. If the financial advisor is only insurance licensed, they will be more biased in recommending the Safe world of investing. There are plenty of advisors who are dually licensed that can offer advice on both topics.

When we meet with prospective clients, we provide them with preliminary retirement income analysis, which helps them contextualize the information needed to make knowledgeable decisions about their money. We develop a retirement income analysis with just about every prospective client that comes into our office, because it is so helpful for individual decision-making. A thorough retirement income analysis gives you a benchmark of the amount of money you can take from your investments on a monthly basis given a certain rate of return and can even show the impact of stock market volatility on your accounts.

Another benefit to the lump sum is flexibility. For example, let's say that in doing this analysis, you determine that in your retirement—to meet all your goals, in addition to what you will be receiving from Social Security and any other income that you may have—you will need $3,000 a month from your retirement funds and lump sum that has now been rolled over into an **IRA**.

We could then illustrate you taking $3,000 a month out of that account. Now let's say a few years later your mortgage is now paid off, and you would like to lower that monthly amount to $2,500. Again, quite simple. You just go ahead and lower the amount you receive to $2,500 a month. As your needs change, the payment is easy to adjust.

Another benefit to being in control of the money is the ability to take extra withdrawals out at your discretion. Let's say you decide to take a nice family vacation and you want an extra $15,000 out of the account. You can withdraw that $15,000 from that **IRA** account you had rolled your pension into without changing the payment amounts. This is another example of control and flexibility, which you would not have if you take the monthly payments from the company and not the lump sum.

One additional potential advantage of the lump sum option is the possibility that you can do considerably better in a good investment environment—if you pick the right investments—than if the money had been invested by the company that holds the pension plan (on the contrary, you could do worse). There is even a possibility that you could even grow the lump sum while taking out the $3,000 each month, or maybe that $15,000 for the vacation comes at a time when the market is doing well, and it comes purely from the gains in the account. In the right investment environment, and with good investment decisions, that lump sum might even double over time.

That does come, however, with a price—you bear the investment risk, and if you are "bad" with money, perhaps it is best that you do not have control over that lump sum of money.

Finally, the biggest advantage to some is that you can pass this lump sum of money on to your children and grandchildren. Since this money was likely rolled into an IRA, if your children inherit it, they can stretch out the IRA over their lifetime, which means they are forced to take small distributions out every year. Each year, the distribution gets a tiny bit bigger, just like a required minimum distribution.

**Please note:* there are proposed rule changes that may eliminate the stretch IRA provision, so there is a significant chance the stretch IRA provision will no longer be an option in the near future.*[6]

The last major disadvantage is that you are potentially adding fuel to the fire on the tax time bomb that is your pre-tax assets. It is not uncommon to have an autoworker retire with $1 million in their 401(k) and $1 million in their lump sum pension. Many times, the spouse has a significant amount saved in pre-tax status as well. Eventually, you will be forced to take distributions from these accounts at whatever tax rates may be at that time. This is something you want to be aware of when taking the lump sum.

Option Two: Monthly Pension Payouts

Now, let's walk through the second option, which is that you leave things as they are, and the company is on the hook to pay you a monthly check as long as you live. Here, too, there are advantages and disadvantages.

First, let's explore the disadvantages. The primary disadvantages are basically the exact opposite of the advantages to taking the lump sum that we just covered. With this option, you completely lack control and flexibility. You can't change the payments up or down. You also limit your potential to do better on the investment side. Any remaining funds when you die cannot become legacy money that passes on for thirty or forty years into the future for children or grandchildren, as it could with an **IRA** as we discussed earlier. This is going to be money that will likely die with you, or with you and your spouse. When you and your spouse are no longer here, these payments come to an end.

There are, however, some positives in choosing to take a monthly payout. The primary advantage is peace of mind. You are guaranteed to get those checks as long as you live, or as long as you and your spouse live. In a lot of cases, there may also be a social security supplement to pay you more in your early years of retirement, if you retire before sixty-two. The payments will keep coming, month after month, very predictably. Logically, this makes the choice more difficult for healthy individuals with long life expectancies, as the company will be bearing more of a risk.

The second advantage is consistency. You are effectively forced to be on a budget, because you can't spend what you don't have. As was mentioned earlier, if you are not the best with money or you are concerned that you may pass away first and are uncertain about what would happen if your spouse inherited the money, you may be better off keeping it in a monthly payment that is guaranteed for the rest of your lives.

There is also an additional negative possibility to consider—if the company goes into bankruptcy. Retirees in the auto industry already lived through this possible reality a decade ago. Should the company that is paying your pension fall into bankruptcy, there is a federal agency, the Pension Benefit Guaranty Corporation (PBGC), which, in effect, has your back.

The PBGC is much like the FDIC, which you are probably more familiar with—and quite comfortable with. You've probably noticed the FDIC logo on the front of every bank, but you're likely less familiar with the PBGC. They work in a similar way. Companies that have pensions pay a premium into the federal government, which in turn ensures that the pension benefits will be paid in the event that the company goes bankrupt.

What type of pension plans does the Pension Benefit Guaranty Corporation stand behind? The answer is: almost all defined benefit plans offered by private sector employers. Defined benefit plans promise to pay you a specific benefit, usually a monthly amount, beginning at retirement and continuing for the rest of your life. According to the PBGC website, currently, about 900,000 retirees in more than 4,600 failed plans receive their pensions through PBGC, even though, for many of them, their companies may no longer be in business. An additional 620,000 workers will receive benefits through that system when they retire.

Below is a table showing the maximum pension benefit guarantees as of 2019:

PBGC Maximum Monthly Guarantees For 2019

Age	Straight-Life	*Joint & 50% Survivor
70	$9,309.20	$8,378.28
69	$8,355.85	$7,520.27
68	$7,514.65	$6,763.19
67	$6,785.62	$6,107.06
66	$6,168.75	$5,551.88
65	$5,607.95	$5,047.16
64	$5,215.39	$4,693.85
63	$4,822.84	$4,340.56
62	$4,430.28	$3,987.25
61	$4,037.72	$3,633.95
60	$3,645.17	$3,280.65
59	$3,420.85	$3,078.77
58	$3,196.53	$2,876.88
57	$2,972.21	$2,674.99
56	$2,747.90	$2,473.11
55	$2,523.58	$2,271.22

*Joint & 50% amounts apply only if both spouses are the same age.

At age sixty-five, on a single life basis, up to $5,607.95 per month is guaranteed. As long as your pension isn't over $5,607.95 per month, it's 100-percent guaranteed by the federal government. If you select joint life, then your guaranteed amount is $5,047.16.

The problem for autoworkers is that they may have a substantial amount of their pension not protected by the PBGC, especially if they retire early. If you retire at age sixty with a $5,000-per-month pension, you could see a reduction down to $3,645 if your company were to fail.

An article from 2009 in the Financial Times entitled "GM shows gravity of pension challenge" highlights this very issue regarding the PBGC maximum:

"Its maximum annual payment is $54,000 for a 65-year-old, but only $20,000 for a 50-year-old. And in Detroit, it is commonplace for car workers to retire on full pension at 50. The PBGC has calculated that if it took over all the auto industry's pensions, members would lose 40 percent on average. A 50-year-old GM pensioner with a $54,000 annual entitlement, Mr. Ralfe reckons, would lose 60 percent. Add that all up, and GM's annual $9bn pension bill would be cut by $3.5bn."[7]

It is important to note that PBGC does not insure three categories of private sector, defined benefit plans: professional service employers with twenty-five or fewer employees, church groups, and defined benefit pension plans sponsored by federal, state, or local governments.

Here in Detroit, we are already familiar with the third category, as the City of Detroit filed for Chapter 9 Bankruptcy on July 18, 2013. The Detroit pensions for the people that work for the City of Detroit were not insured by PBGC.

That's why it was such a serious matter when Detroit declared bankruptcy and the municipal workers who were promised pensions—and may have already begun to collect pensions—faced huge cuts to their benefits because there was no insurance. General workers suffered a 4.5-percent base cut in pensions and the elimination of an annual cost-of-living increase. The pensions of police and firefighters weren't cut, but an annual 2.25-percent cost-of-living adjustment was reduced to about 1 percent.[8]

Hopefully, this section has alleviated any concern and misunderstanding about the general safety of pension payments if you opt not to take a lump sum. Because of the Pension Benefit Guaranty Corporation, there are sound protections for most pensions, and clear employment situations where PBGC protections do not apply.

Case Study

To provide a real-life example of a couple who considered this choice, lump sum versus monthly payouts, it is worthwhile to walk through our work with a client—a husband and wife we'll call Ron and Kathy—who considered with us the choices they had, and what would be the best strategy in their particular circumstances.

Ron was retiring at age sixty-eight from one of the Big Three automotive companies and had worked as an engineer for over thirty years. His wife was a nurse and was retiring at the same time as Ron.

His first option was to take a lump sum for approximately $1 million dollars. Or, he could take a life annuity of $5,700 per month for the rest of his life.

Another choice was to take what is described as a 65% joint and survivor pension, which means that he could start out receiving $5,350 a month; and if he died, Kathy would receive $3,477 per month for the rest of her life. He was leaning toward the 65% survivor option until we examined what could be done if he took the lump sum of $1 million and rolled it over into an **IRA**.

Specific to this couple was the fact that Kathy worked in the medical profession and would receive a pension of her own on top of her social security benefit since she retired at the same time as Ron. Add to that, when Ron turned seventy in two more years, he would turn his full social security benefit on, and their expenses would be covered without even touching his pension!

The moral of the story is that every circumstance is unique, and the retirement income analysis differs for every individual.

What we were able to do with Ron and Kathy, when all was said and done, was to have them take control of the money by electing to take the lump sum instead of taking the monthly payout. Even though the monthly payout was somewhat attractive, Ron determined that he did not really need all the income on a monthly basis that they were offering from the pension, and he preferred control over the lump sum.

Secondly, he now has all the flexibility. He consolidated his 401(k) and the pension plan and rolled them over into one bucket, his **IRA**.

It has been allocated in a variety of strategies with varying risk tolerances. He has a portion of the money in deferred annuities that will provide guaranteed income in the future without stock market risk, and he is taking some income from that when needed.

Additionally, he has some money exposed in the traditional well-balanced stock and bond portfolios that we typically build for clients. With that blend, we are targeting a rate of return of 5 to 7 percent net of all expenses (of course, there is no guarantee of future results). It could well be higher, but let's say 5 to 7 percent, which is more than enough to generate what would have been the pension income, and he has control over the entire lump sum.

More importantly to Ron and Kathy is that this money will likely pass on to their kids and grandchildren. They were excited to see what type of inheritance they might be able to leave behind if they were to let this money grow over the remainder of their lifetimes.

Your Pension, Your Choice

What it boils down to is that there is no overarching answer, no one-size-fits-all decision when the choice is between taking a lump sum or monthly payouts for your pension benefit. We have laid out for you in this chapter the positives and negatives of each choice. It's up to you and your financial advisor to balance the pros and cons and make the decision that is most suitable for you.

In most instances, the positives outweigh the potential negatives in selecting to take the lump sum. But this is a choice that should be made based on your own unique circumstances and situation.

Individual circumstances matter—in fact, they are what matters most. We suggest that you get individualized advice from a member of our firm or some other qualified person that you trust and feel comfortable with, so that you can decide what's best for you and your family.

CHAPTER 4

WHAT ARE THE FUNDAMENTAL FACTORS TO MAKING THIS DECISION?

"Be true to yourself and your values."

– Alan Mulally

What factors should you think about, and in what order, so that you can make the best decision? Here is our suggestion of an effective way to proceed. There are five basic steps and questions that will help you through the decision-making process as you evaluate whether to take a lump sum and roll it over into an Individual Retirement Account (which means you don't have to take any money at all right away unless you're over 70.5 years old), or begin taking the monthly payout from your company.

#1: **Do I Need the Additional Income?**

Like the example of Ron and Kathy, question number one is a great question to start with. If you do not need this money, or maybe you need only a portion of the monthly income your pension would provide, then it presents a wonderful opportunity to pass money on to your children. If you don't need the monthly income, then you should probably roll the money over. Or maybe you only need a portion of the lump sum to generate income. In which case, you can roll it over, split it into two buckets, with one bucket generating income and the other focused on long-term growth.

On the other hand, if you absolutely need the money—and need the maximum monthly payouts—then that may sway your decision in the opposite direction, toward proceeding with the monthly payments. So, the first question you need to ask and answer is: do I need the additional income?

#2: **Am I Responsible With Money?**

The second question that you should ask yourself—and answer—is: am I responsible with money? We've found that for most autoworkers, the answer is yes. You've worked long and hard and been loyal to your company for years, possibly decades. Most retirees who have put in that level of effort to accumulate a six- or seven-figure portfolio understand the value of a dollar. They understand retirement is not the time to take big risks. They saw firsthand how devastating a recession can be; they understand uncertainty.

But you still must ask yourself this question and be honest with yourself. You need to make sure you're responsible with money and disciplined in following through on your financial plan, long term.

Here's why: Let's say you roll the money over, after a financial advisor has created a detailed long-term plan for you, in which you have decided that a good withdrawal rate on that money is 4 percent, for example. So, you are taking out enough money each month, consistent with the plan you decided upon based on your needs, totaling approximately 4 percent per year.

Then, you start spending wildly for whatever reason—buying that Corvette you've always wanted, a cottage up north, a vacation home in Florida, and on top of that you're helping your kids out with their expenses, and so on. Your advisor warns you that you are way over budget, but after all, it's your money, and they cannot stop you from spending it.

Money that was supposed to last a lifetime can quickly disappear. That is why the second question is, am I responsible with money?

#3: Can I Trust Someone to Invest My Money?

Next, you should ask yourself, can I trust someone to invest my money to generate an income and preserve principal?

This may not be true for everybody, but most people are much better off working with a financial advisor than attempting to navigate the ups and downs of the investment process themselves. Every year, DALBAR comes out with a study entitled the "Quantitative Analysis of Investor Behavior." [9]

Each year, it continues to prove that humans make for terrible investors. At times of stress in the markets, we act emotionally and irrationally. At times of euphoria in the markets, we also act emotionally and irrationally.

This can all be summed up by the following fact: **the average asset-allocated investor has not even beat inflation over the last thirty years:**

	Average Equity Fund Investor (%)	Average Fixed Income Fund Investor (%)	Average Asset Allocation Fund Investor (%)	S&P 500 (%)	Bloomberg-Barclays Aggregate Bond Index (%)	Inflation (%)
30 Year	4.09%	0.26%	1.79%	9.97%	6.10%	2.49%
20 Year	3.88%	0.22%	1.87%	5.62%	4.55%	2.17%
10 Year	9.66%	0.70%	4.53%	13.12%	3.48%	1.82%
5 Year	3.96%	-0.40%	1.50%	8.49%	2.52%	1.56%
3 Year	5.58%	-0.11%	1.84%	9.26%	2.06%	2.04%
12 Month	-9.42%	-2.84%	-6.97%	-4.38%	0.01%	1.93%

To summarize this point, an investor's biggest hindrance to investment success is their behavior in times of stress <u>or</u> when things are going really well. When things are going well, fear of missing out kicks in, and investors decide to put more money at risk, because they don't want to miss out on the gains their neighbor has been talking about non-stop.

When things are going poorly, they panic, and they sell out of the market. It is very easy to say, in a calm moment while reading this book, "Well, I know the market will always come back. I won't do that." We're here to tell you, based on our experience, that most people cannot control themselves.

One thing we like to say at our firm is that the market can drop 10 to 20 percent at any time, for no reason whatsoever. It can be gut-wrenching to see your nest-egg drop 10 percent, or even 5 percent, and it is hard to keep your composure and not make a move. Thus, most people are better off working with someone who can coach them through these turbulent times. Or, if you're the type that would fire an advisor for a small loss, maybe you're better off taking the monthly payouts.

Let's think back to Chapter 2, when we discussed the top hundred companies with the largest pension obligations; **their pension investments were down on average by 3.53 percent in 2018.** That's the best of the best of the investment managers in the world, so please don't hire a financial advisor thinking they will provide positive returns year in and year out, regardless of where the market is going. Also important to note is that the average asset allocation investor was down almost 7 percent in 2018, more than the S&P 500.

There will be years when you're down, and if you accept the premise that most people are better off working with a financial advisor, and you believe that applies to you, then you need to identify someone you can trust. We'll discuss more about how to find a financial advisor you can trust in Chapter 8.

#4: How Will This Decision Affect My Family?

When you pass on, is it going to hurt your children that because you took a monthly payout—and now all of a sudden that has ended—you are unable to leave them anything? Especially if you had wanted to leave something to the kids and grandkids? Or perhaps it's a charity that you've supported your whole life, and you were looking to leave more to that cause.

On the other hand, what if you opt to take the lump sum, but you spend it wildly or invest it poorly, and you run out of money in retirement? That will certainly affect your loved ones, because now they must bail out Mom and Dad. That is why it is important to consider: how will this decision affect those I love?

#5: How Is My Health (and My Spouse's Health)?

As we discussed in Chapter 1, longevity is increasing on average. Companies use the law of large numbers and can predict the average longevity of their retirees accurately.

The only advantage you may have over them is insider information on your health. If you know, or at least believe, that you have some sort of health ailment that will prevent you from meeting your life expectancy, it may be in your best interest to take the lump sum. If something happens to you, this money lives on. It either supports your spouse, transfers to your children, or passes on to another beneficiary of your choosing.

But you may also have to consider your spouse, and it may be wise to take the monthly payments even if you are in poor health, as you can still elect a survivor option for them.

Those are the five fundamental questions that you should be able to answer to help you make the choice as to whether to take a lump sum or monthly payments in retirement. For some of those questions, it can be tremendously helpful to get outside input from a financial professional who customarily works with retirees—someone you feel comfortable with, and who will provide you with truthful answers and honest input. That can make all the difference in the world, as you decide which option is best for you. To briefly review, here are the five questions that you ought to answer before you move forward with a decision on whether to take a lump sum or monthly payments in retirement:

1. Do I need additional income?
2. Am I responsible with money?
3. Can I trust someone to invest my money and generate an income and preserve principal?
4. When I die, how will this decision affect those I love?
5. How is my health (and my spouse's health)?

As you consider what to do first in working through whether to choose to take the lump sum retirement payment your company is offering, or the monthly payments for life, the answers to these questions will help guide your decision.

CHAPTER 5

HOW DO I INCORPORATE MY 401(K) WITH MY PENSION LUMP SUM?

"A car is thirty thousand parts you're putting together."

– Mary Barra

Most autoworkers, no matter what division they're in, can agree with the simple fact that things tend to get more complicated over time. Whether it's the engine, touch display, product design, or supply chain, it's likely a bit more complicated than it was decades ago. Heck, you practically need a computer engineering degree to change the air in your tires now.

The same with investing. Today's world of investing is much more complicated than it was twenty or thirty years ago. The sheer amount of investment types (stocks, bonds, annuities, alternatives, ETFs, mutual funds, closed end funds, CDs, REITs, etc.) and strategies (active, passive, international, dynamic, tactical, etc.) can be overwhelming. We are at all-time highs in the market and near all-time lows in interest rates, which makes for a tumultuous investing environment, especially if you don't know what you're doing. Traditional fixed income will not provide the same stability that it's provided over the past thirty years if we do in fact enter a prolonged rising-interest-rate environment.

If you take the pension, there's a good chance your monthly income will be covered by the pension combined with social security. This makes investing the 401(k) a bit simpler. A nice diversified blend of stocks and bonds might do just fine, which could be accomplished within the 401(k) funds or by rolling it to an IRA.

It gets a lot trickier when you take the lump sum, as you have transferred the investment risk of the lump sum to yourself.

Now, you need to invest it like your company would. Are they going to carry large, single-stock holdings? No! They are going to create a nice diversified blend to minimize the volatility and focus on risk-adjusted return. This means, on a year-to-year basis, there will always be several asset classes doing better than your overall return.

You may also look to incorporate an annuity, just like some of the larger companies have offloaded their pension liabilities to annuity companies. This is the same exact thing, albeit on a much smaller scale. This reduces the investment burden that you transferred to yourself, as you turned around and transferred some of it to the insurance company.

There are rules of thumb that say invest your age in bonds and safe vehicles like a fixed or fixed indexed annuity. For instance, if you are sixty-five, this would mean you should have 65 percent of your portfolio in fixed instruments, as you are looking to phase away from the ups and downs of stocks as you age. This can vary significantly from person to person and should only be used as a conversation starter.

In the retirement-planning world, we often use the analogy of climbing a mountain to explain saving for retirement. As you work, you save and save, amassing a sizable 401(k) and other savings. When climbing a mountain, you climb and climb and eventually reach the summit. For retirees, the summit is your retirement. It took a lot of work to get there, but you actually have to be more careful getting down the mountain.

Think about it that for a moment: At retirement, in theory, you might possibly have the most money of your life. Add in a pension lump sum, and this could have the effect of doubling your life savings in an instant.

A mistake at this point in your life can be devastating. Whether it's allocating too much to stocks, or sitting on the sidelines with cash, missteps at this point in the game are hard to recover from.

Rolling Over the 401(k)

Generally, once the client reaches age 59.5, we recommend doing a direct rollover from the 401(k) to an IRA. A direct rollover is paid directly to the new institution rather than a check being cut to you.

Once the rollover is complete, you can invest however you please, and are no longer restricted to the fund lineup provided by your company. This could be any type of combination of stocks, bonds, mutual funds, ETFs, cash, real estate, annuities, alternatives, and so on.

Many times, your 401(k) may be made up of a variety of different tax structures. Perhaps you contributed to a Roth 401(k) once that was available. Maybe you made after-tax contributions one year, and you have growth on those contributions. This means you would need to open both an IRA and a Roth IRA to complete a rollover. The most confusing of the bunch is after-tax contributions, of which the contributions can be rolled into a Roth IRA and the gains on the contributions must be rolled into an IRA. Again, this is something unique to each individual, and it's something you want to carefully evaluate to make sure it's done correctly.

Once you are 59.5, you can withdrawal from an IRA without penalty. Prior to that age, you have to be careful. If a client retires after fifty-five, they would typically be eligible to withdraw out of their 401(k) and avoid the 10 percent penalty. Therefore, many times when a client retires within this window, we may opt to leave a designated sum of money inside the 401(k) while rolling a portion over to an IRA. The last thing you want to do is pay a penalty and give the government more money than necessary.

A word of caution prior to executing a rollover: **Carefully evaluate your company stock.**

In our opinion, if you are holding more than 3 to 5 percent of your portfolio in your company's stock, you are opening yourself up to unnecessary risk. Unnecessary risk is one of the more-often-made mistakes when it comes to creating a retirement income plan. Loyalty is all well and good, but you must think of yourself first. We've seen plenty of clients who come in with their whole 401(k) in company stock! The only thing this ensures is that if the company goes under, you're not only unemployed now, but you're broke as well.

In all seriousness, company stock can be dangerous. But this doesn't necessarily mean run out and sell all your stock, especially if it's inside your 401(k). There is a provision for this stock called *Net Unrealized Appreciation*. This is a special tax advantage for highly appreciated stock inside your 401(k). It allows you to take a distribution of your company stock from your pre-tax 401(k) to an after-tax brokerage account, which would cause a taxable event of the basis and allow any gains to be reported at more friendly capital gains rates versus ordinary income (IRA withdrawals are taxed as ordinary income).

Let's look at an example:

Say, in 2009, you bought $17,000 worth of Ford stock at $1.70 per share, so you purchased 10,000 shares. For simplicity, let's say you bought no further shares, and you retire a decade later and Ford stock is now at $12 per share, or $120,000. The Net Unrealized Appreciation provision would allow you to take all that stock out of your 401(k) and move it to an after-tax account, and all you would have to do is pay tax on the $17,000 you originally invested. Anytime you sell the stock thereafter, you would owe capital gains tax on it, which is more favorable than ordinary income rates.

Please consult with a tax professional if you feel you may be eligible for this provision.

Putting a Plan in Place

Before you make any decisions regarding your retirement, we can't stress the importance enough of having a solid retirement income analysis and income projection prepared for you to carefully consider. Having that done is, in our view, essential to sound decision-making.

As part of our Retirement Roadmap Review at Richard W. Paul & Associates, we call this our Retirement Analyzer, where we crunch all of your numbers and project out what your retirement might look like at a conservative growth rate and a variety of factors unique to your situation—the size of your 401(k) and other assets, pension or lump sum, expenses, RMDs, taxes, social security, and more.

For many of our automotive clients, we run this analysis both ways, and it will look drastically different for each scenario.

We suggest that you have an analysis like this done with a financial advisor who has specific expertise in the retirement planning area and works predominantly with retirees like yourself. We suggest this because they are much more likely to know about real-life circumstances that an online program just can't spit out or doesn't know to ask you. Perhaps you want to see how your portfolio could sustain a spending shock, such as a long-term care event, or an extended period where the market performs poorly.

Having a retirement income analysis done will let you know three essential elements of a sound decision.

First, it will let you know, based on your goals of how much income you want—factoring in all the other elements—if you have enough money to last for the rest of your life.

Here's basically how it works. You tell us how much monthly income you want. Let's say that it is $10,000 a month. We then run the numbers, factor in inflation and other variables, and tell you whether you are likely to be okay financially through age ninety-five or one hundred. You can see how important it is to know, as you make this decision, whether you will still have money available to you from your retirement at those ages. That would certainly indicate that you're in a good financial position. If you're being unrealistic and want $15,000 per month and your portfolio can't sustain that . . . well, that's information you need to know.

Second, it will help you to determine the rate of return you will need over the long-term. Just like your company would have to assume a rate of return on their investment assets to fund their pension obligations, we must assume a rate of return on your investment assets. We must be careful not to be too aggressive with this number, because it does no good to run a retirement analysis assuming a consistent 8 percent return. Sure, you could possibly get 8 percent over the next few decades, but we like to be conservative and cautious with this number, as we don't know what the future holds.

Lastly, it gives you an idea of what you might leave your beneficiaries at given life expectancies. Maybe, when you look at the numbers, you might say to yourself that you're leaving too much money behind and you want to spend more! Believe it or not, this is not uncommon whatsoever. You worked hard for your money and should have the ability to enjoy your retirement to its fullest.

Doing a thorough analysis now gives you the opportunity to have these discussions prior to making your lump sum decision. It also gives you a much better idea how the outside assets can be used in combination with either the lump sum or the monthly payments. The results of a retirement income analysis can help you to arrive at an answer that is right for you and your particular circumstances, needs, and objectives.

CHAPTER 6

WHAT ARE THE KEY PLANNING OPPORTUNITIES TO CONSIDER?

"Thinking is the hardest work there is, which is probably the reason so few engage in it."

– Henry Ford

The major risk in taking the lump sum is that you lose that lifetime income guarantee—the check that arrives every month, like clockwork. This can be offset if you take some of the money and buy an annuity with a similar income guarantee, which would provide the predictable monthly income on that piece of your retirement lump sum. That is why many people, and let's use that million-dollar example again, might roll over the entire $1 million into an IRA, and then take a half-million dollars, 50 percent of that, and put it into an annuity where they would receive an income guarantee. They can rely on that income, month after month, for the rest of their lives, and they also have control over the $500,000. Some people view this as the best of both worlds, financially speaking.

When it comes to the different types of annuities, it's similar to types of cars. There are sports cars, SUVs, luxury cars, fuel-efficient cars, etc. With annuities, there are just as many options, if not more. There are simple ones, complicated ones, safe annuities, risky annuities, income-oriented annuities, immediate annuities, deferred annuities, and on and on. Just like with a car, you can add a variety of features to it. Think of it this way: When you add the sunroof and technology package, it's going to add to the cost of the car, but also give you some features you get to enjoy. The same can be said with an annuity—you can add lifetime income riders or healthcare features to customize it to your wants and needs.

One major misconception with annuities is that many people seem to think you lose access to your principal. In some cases, this is true. You lose access to your principal when you annuitize the contract, which means you've elected lifetime income payments (or payments over a different set term).

Many people do not want this, and there's a good chance you don't want to lose access to the principal if you're taking the lump sum, since your pension would act like an annuitized annuity if you were to take the monthly payments. Therefore, annuity companies have added income features that allow you to take a lifetime income without the need to annuitize right away—this is referred to as an income rider.

Of course, this is an oversimplification, but the idea here is that it can be difficult finding the right annuity for you. When dealing with pension money, we would tend to prefer the safer, fixed vehicles, which don't participate in market losses.

On the contrary, when you take the lifetime payments, you're better protected against poor spending decisions. In other words, you protect yourself from yourself.

This approach could also provide a potentially higher payout rate than trying to replicate this on your own with an insurance company. You may also receive a social security supplement if you retire before age sixty-two. This alone might sway your decision, as you may not be able to match this supplemental income payout with an annuity if you were to take the lump sum. It is important to consult a financial advisor who has expertise in annuities to compare an annuity payout from an insurance company to the payout guaranteed by the company.

Let's take a moment to compare the payout rate from your pension against the lump sum that we outlined earlier in this chapter. Let's say, again, that you have a $1 million lump sum, versus a payout rate of $6,000 a month. The payout of $6,000 a month equals $72,000 a year. Therefore, the cash flow payout rate on that $1 million is 7.2 percent. That may be a higher guaranteed payout rate than you can get elsewhere.

That is why you should compare the rate to what you might be able to get if you invest the money. Although by taking the monthly pension payout you have given up control of the money, the positive, or reward, is that you remove your downside risk. The negative, or downside, of taking that monthly payment amount is your loss of flexibility. You no longer have control over the assets. You cannot pass the money on, and you limit your investment upside.

Let's go through each of those risks and rewards.

First, there's the loss of flexibility. If you take a monthly payout, you don't have any flexibility in the payments, nor do you have upside or downside with the investments. You no longer have an asset you can pass on, because there is not an asset. Rather, there is a stream of payments guaranteed for your and possibly your spouse's life.

Second, because you don't have an asset that you are able to reach, you limit your investment upside. You are merely going to receive monthly payments. If you roll that money over and invest it at a higher rate than the payout amount, you could ultimately amass a much larger amount of money.

Here is a quick-and-easy chart that lists the pros and cons of the monthly pension payout and the lump sum rollover:

The Lump Sum	
Pros:	Cons:
Control and flexibility	You bear the investment risk
Ability to pass on the money to children and grandchildren	You forego the lifetime income guarantee
Potential to do better by investing the money	Potential early withdrawal penalty prior to age 59.5

The Monthly Payments	
Pros:	Cons:
Guaranteed lifetime income	No control over principal
You protect yourself from poor spending/investing decisions	You cannot pass on the asset to beneficiaries or charities

Four Planning Opportunities to Consider

#1: Retiring Prior to 59.5

For those fortunate to retire at an early age, this opportunity presents some unique challenges. If you retire after age 55, you can take withdrawals from your 401(k) and avoid the 10 percent early withdrawal penalty. Therefore, if you rolled your lump sum into an IRA, you could let this IRA money defer to age 59.5 and use the 401(k) to bridge the gap until you reach that age.

If you retire before age 55, that's another story. Any withdrawals from either account will be subject to the 10 percent penalty, unless they meet certain exclusions. Like any IRA, you can avoid the 10 percent penalty for certain hardships or higher education costs for you or your dependents. But the challenge that retirees of this age face is that they need income to live off of. This is where an important provision in Internal Revenue Code (IRC) Section 72, part t, comes into play.

This provision is more commonly referred to as the 72(t) provision. The 72(t) allows you to take a Series of Substantially Equal

Periodic Payments (SOSEPP) from your IRA prior to age 59.5 without penalty. The dollar amount has to meet one of the three calculation methods (required minimum distribution, fixed amortization, or fixed annuitization). The payments must continue for a minimum of five years and must go until at least age 59.5. This is something that needs to be carefully planned for, as you cannot change it once it's set. If you change it or stop it prior to meeting the requisite timeframes, all distributions will be penalized!

Please consult with a tax professional if you feel you may be eligible for this provision.

#2: Reducing Your Future Tax Liability

Let's look at Bob, an engineer who is retiring from GM at age sixty-two. He has built up $900,000 in his 401(k), he has $100,000 in his bank account, and he has decided to take his pension lump sum for $1 million. Bob doesn't need a heck of a lot of money to live off of with his wife still working, and he's also considering starting social security so he doesn't need to take income from his portfolio.

Bob is now in an interesting predicament, having 95 percent of his money in pre-tax status. You can bet your bottom dollar that Uncle Sam has his eyes on Bob. At age 70.5, he'll be forced to take distributions, which will require him to pay income tax at whatever tax rates are at that time. Say his $1.9 million in pre-tax money grows by 5 percent annually over the next eight years—his forced distribution (or required minimum distribution) would be over $100,000!

But now that Bob is retired and his salary has fallen off, he has an opportunity to convert some of his pre-tax IRA money to tax-free Roth IRA money through Roth Conversions. This is as simple as shifting the money from one account to the other and paying the tax bill in the year of the conversion (thus, locking in today's tax rates). If taxes were to go up in the future, the money that's been converted to a Roth IRA would be protected from the future tax increases. It would also reduce the amount of forced distributions he would have to take at age 70.5, since RMDs are not required on Roth IRA money.

Now, that doesn't mean Bob should convert all $1.9 million at once, as this would drive him into the highest tax brackets. But putting a systematic plan in place to convert a portion of the money on a year-to-year basis may put him in a much more favorable planning situation down the road.

Not only could this put Bob in a better position, but it could put Bob's beneficiaries in a better position. Let's say Bob has two children, and Bob and his wife both pass away at age eighty-five. His children would then be able to take the Roth portion tax-free, but for the IRAs they would have to take required distributions on an annual basis, which gets added into their income. Keep in mind, their children will likely be in their prime working years, making more than they've ever made (a.k.a. the government knows what they're doing!).

Please consult with appropriate tax and financial professionals prior to implementing a Roth Conversion strategy.

#3: Inflation

Let's go all the way back to the $64,000 Question reference we discussed in the introduction of this book.

Interestingly enough, we plugged in $64,000 from back when the phrase originated in 1942. In today's dollars, that amount is now worth approximately $1 million when adjusted for inflation, as you can see on the chart on the following page:

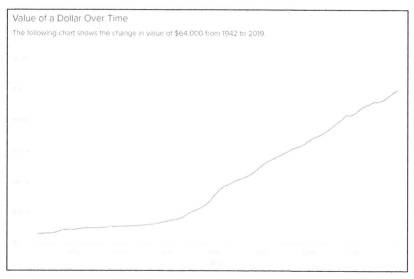

That's inflation for you. You don't notice it on a year-to-year basis, but when you give it enough time to build, it can have resounding effects on your nest egg and your retirement.

It can also have a resounding effect on your pension. Let's say you retired in the year 2000 with a $5,000-per-month pension. You would need almost $7,500 in today's dollars to match that same buying power you had in the year 2000.

Unfortunately, most pensions today do not come with a Cost of Living Adjustment (COLA), which helps the pension income to keep up with inflation. If a pension lacks this feature, that means your income stream is being devalued each year, even though you don't even notice, because your payment stays the same. That's why we call inflation the silent killer.

As we talked about in previous chapters, one option when taking the lump sum is to put a portion of the funds into an annuity that could provide a pension-like stream of income. Some insurance companies allow you to take this income with an increasing payment option, which would help protect you from inflation eating away at the buying power of your income.

Another option, of course, would be to invest a portion into the market for long-term growth, so you have a bucket of money to turn to when needed for additional buying power.

#4: Long-Term Care Planning

We could spend a whole chapter on this topic, but the short version is that long-term care is a hole in a lot of retirement plans. According to longtermcare.gov, someone turning sixty-five today has almost a 70-percent chance of needing some type of long-term care services and support in their remaining years.

There are three primary ways to plan for long-term care:

i. Long-Term Care Insurance

This is not the most exciting option, but it's a simple way to plan for these costs. If you are older, have an illness, or have a family history, you may not be insurable. In our opinion, the ideal time to get a Long-Term Care Insurance (LTC) policy is in your late fifties or early sixties.

We've found that most people don't like paying a monthly

premium for something they may or may not use, especially when it costs as much as these policies. It seems that most people who have a long-term care policy have witnessed firsthand how devastating the costs of a long-term care event can be. There are certain provisions that need to be discussed with a qualified financial professional to factor in premium increases, cost-of-living adjustments, etc.

Either way, if you take the lump sum or monthly payments, you'll have the option to then purchase long-term care insurance to help plan for those future costs.

ii. Self-Insuring

Self-insuring can be a nice option for those who take the lump sum. This involves setting a bucket of money aside and letting it grow and grow. If it's not needed for long-term care costs, it then passes on to your children.

The big question for the self-insuring option is: how much do you need? Healthcare costs vary depending on your location and type of care. Here in Michigan, the 2018 median cost for a semi-private nursing home was $8,562 per month, with in-home healthcare being about half that cost, at $4,195 per month.[10]

Take an $8,562-per-month cost and expand that over three years, and you're paying over $300,000 for your healthcare needs. Project that out a couple decades, and that number could easily reach upwards $500,000 at its current inflation trajectory.

iii. Healthcare Riders on Annuities or Life Insurance

Most people want to avoid Medicaid at all costs. The government doesn't want you to go on Medicaid either, as it's expensive for them.

As part of the Pension Protection Act of 2006, Congress enacted an incentive to keep you off Medicaid and provide additional coverage for healthcare costs, introducing healthcare riders as an additional feature to a life insurance or annuity policy. Life insurance pays a lump sum at death, and annuities pay a stream of income while you are living. These extra features can be added to annuities and life insurance policies to allow you early access to the death benefit or to enhance your income if a long-term care event occurs. Since there is no underwriting for annuity contracts, these healthcare riders can be very attractive for those with existing medical issues.

With life insurance, many people like the concept of purchasing the insurance for wealth transfer, understanding that they have access to a portion of the death benefit if they end up needing it for long-term care.

This tends to be an appealing option for many retirees, because it doesn't have the use-it-or-lose-it provision like typical LTC insurance. If you don't need the income enhancement on your annuity, it would still generate income over your lifetime. If you don't need the accelerated death benefit on your life insurance, that's great—the death benefit then goes to your heirs tax-free.

Again, there are a variety of ways this can be structured, and if this is something you may be interested in, please consult with a financial professional.

CHAPTER 7

WHAT ARE THE THINGS NOT TO DO?

> *"Most people spend more time and energy going around problems than in trying to solve them."*
> – Henry Ford

We imagine that by this point you are getting a good sense of how important this decision is—and that it does not need to be an overly complicated decision. Our hope is that if you felt overwhelmed prior to picking up this book, your apprehension has started to subside. The goal here is to provide you with enough information to help you to confidently make the decision that's right for you and your family. As much as that means suggesting what you ought to do, it also means alerting you to what not to do.

There are six things that could quite possibly impact your future decision in a negative way. These admonitions are all based in real experiences—people have made these mistakes, and they have actually done what is described below.

#1: Don't Overthink It – Engineers, We're Talking to You!

Even if you're smarter than most people, you shouldn't expect to figure out a methodology that a huge, publicly traded company with the help of outside consultants has somehow missed. We've seen it time and time again, spreadsheet after spreadsheet.

As you ponder your pension decision, we would exercise caution on checking with your colleagues who have an affinity for Excel spreadsheets. It is not a good idea to sit with them to compare spreadsheets on the various pension payout options, with various growth rates, to attempt to beat the system.

If you look at the payout options from a mathematical standpoint, because life expectancy is involved, they are all equal from an actuarial standpoint. You are not going to create a spreadsheet that makes you smarter than almost every insurance company in the United States. There is only one surefire way to beat the system, and that's to live longer than they anticipate.

Of course, they have the law of large numbers on their side. Since you are making an isolated decision, this increases your risk versus when there are a lot of people in the pool. It is not at all beneficial or helpful to create a complex spreadsheet and attempt to figure out what the best option may be.

#2: Avoid the Herd Mentality

As we've said in each chapter of this book, this is a highly personalized decision. What's right for you may not be right for the next person. Asking your co-workers about the pension decision they are going to make, in the belief that if most people are doing something it is probably the right thing to do, is a mistake.

In fact, in the investment world, sometimes it's best to do the opposite of what everyone else is doing.

This decision is yours to make, based on your own unique circumstances. It must be the right choice for you and your family. Your family is different and distinct from the people you are talking with, no matter how similar they may seem. As professionals in this business for many years, we have seen people blindsided over and over again because they make what they believe is the safe choice only because it is the most popular opinion.

#3: Don't Rely on What Google Tells You

The internet can be a scary place. We'd bet any medical professional would echo those same thoughts. Have you ever had an illness and searched your symptoms on Google? If you have, you know how overexaggerated and misleading the internet can be. You have a fever and a cough, but you stumble across a page that's telling you that you only have weeks to live.

Googling the words "pension lump sum vs. pension payments" is not the way to decide what to do. Likely, the first five results are paid-for ads from some of the large brokerage firms and insurance firms in the area. You will be hit with what appears to be valid advice from so-called experts that, truth be told, may have no business giving financial advice and likely have considerably less money than you, or by financial planners trying to sell you a product.

Even if the advice is valid, be sure to tread carefully. Remember, there is no silver-bullet solution to this decision—you need to receive individualized advice, not generic advice from a website or online forum.

#4: Don't Think That It's a Scam or a Trick

Part of the reason we spent so much time explaining what goes into the pension decision from the company's perspective, is to alleviate the concern that they're out to get you.

Many retirees facing this decision are under the impression their company is trying to rip them off. In our opinion, it's quite the opposite. We feel these companies are doing their best to fulfill the promises that they've made to you.

#5: Don't Freak Out or Tighten Up

Yes, it is an important financial decision that will have an impact on the rest of your life, but you do not want to freak out. Many times, this is a decision you have to make very quickly. It may not even be your choice to retire.

This can be a time of major stress, but please don't get so nervous and so uptight about this decision that your ability to make the best decision for you and your family becomes clouded.

Having perspective can help. For most people, the decision at hand is only one part of an overall retirement plan. For most people reading this book, there is a more comprehensive financial portfolio, which may include brokerage accounts, 401(k)s, and other savings, and you will also begin to receive Social Security payments.

#6: Don't Act Without a Plan

Having a clear vision of your future is the single most important factor in making this decision.

The biggest mistake you can make is to make an impulse decision without thinking it through. We've had clients come in at fifty-five years of age who consolidated their 401(k) and pension lump sum into a single IRA, without a plan to generate income. Had they consulted us prior, we would have had them leave some assets in their 401(k), as they would have had access to these funds without an early withdrawal penalty, since they retired at age fifty-five. There are still ways to access these IRA funds, but you lose the flexibility of withdrawing at your leisure.

This is a big decision. You need to take a deep breath, remain calm, and really think it through. However, don't drive yourself spreadsheet crazy. Consult a financial planner and make sure that whatever path you take leads to a comfortable retirement.

CHAPTER 8

HOW CAN I FIND A FINANCIAL ADVISOR TO HELP WITH ALL OF THIS?

"Trouble shared is trouble halved."

- Lee Iacocca

One of the benefits of working in the auto industry is the ability to test and drive their cars without having to go car shopping. For those not in the auto industry, every few years we have the fun task of shopping around for a new car. The reason people dislike shopping for cars is the feeling that they're being sold something.

Many people dread meeting with a financial advisor for this very reason. Understandably so, as it isn't easy to find a financial professional these days. Oh, there are plenty of us out there—but it's becoming increasingly difficult to find an individual or firm you know you can trust.

First, there's the confusing collection of certifications we call "designation soup." Then, there's the current contentious debate over fiduciary vs. suitability standards. And to top it off, we have the "testimonial rule" in the Investment Advisers Act, which says Registered Investment Advisors can't directly or indirectly distribute an advertisement that includes a client testimonial or a client's endorsement. So, we can't give out a list of references or ask our clients for an online review.

This all means it's up to individuals to do some research if they want to find an experienced, knowledgeable, and honest financial professional to handle their retirement planning.

Here are seven steps that can help put you on the right track:

#1: Look for a Firm That Can Provide Comprehensive Services

Some firms specialize in one product or service. Look for a firm that can provide you with a holistic plan that offers a variety of services and financial vehicles from which to choose. Firms that offer comprehensive services, or that partner with qualified professionals to provide the services they may not be able to offer, can incorporate more aspects of your financial life into your overall strategy.

As we mentioned in the earlier chapters, an insurance-only licensed advisor could recommend an annuity, but not securities. A securities licensed advisor could recommend securities and not annuities. A dually licensed advisor can recommend both—therefore, you are more likely to get an unbiased recommendation from someone who has both arrows in the quiver.

#2: Make Sure Your Philosophies Align

There are different types of financial professionals with many different specialties. Most focus on wealth accumulation—investing and growing your assets while you're still working. When you're near or in retirement, though, you'll want to find an individual or firm that specializes in preservation and distribution. They should be experienced in protecting your assets and producing an income that will last your lifetime. They should understand tax-efficient strategies and how to hedge against inflation. And they should do legacy and estate planning, or work closely with an attorney who does.

Some financial professionals also have subspecialties; they focus on the unique needs of widows, divorcees, small-business owners, and others. To be sure that the person you're working with understands your needs, you'll have to ask the right questions. We suggest meeting with a few financial professionals or firms so you can find the right fit.

#3: Work With a Fiduciary

The Department of Labor's fiduciary rule, which requires financial professionals to look out for the best interests of their clients when working with qualified funds (money set aside for retirement on a pre-tax basis), began implementation in mid-2017, but ultimately fell through and did not go into effect. This means many financial advising firms are not operating as fiduciaries, meaning they are not required to operate in your best interest. When you're dealing with such a significant sum of money, it only makes sense to get the best possible advice, and the fiduciary standard helps to ensure just that.

A financial professional who works under the suitability standard can use just a handful of factors to make a recommendation—such as your age, risk tolerance and net worth—and the recommendation is not required to work in your best interest. That's not to say that those financial professionals who are held to a suitability standard don't look out for the interest of their clients, but those held to a fiduciary standard are legally obligated to do so.

#4: Choose an Independent Advisor

Some financial professionals contract with and operate under the umbrella of a larger firm that creates and sells financial products and services. Others are actual employees of those firms. Independent financial advisors, on the other hand, are not affiliated with any company, bank, or other corporate entity, so they aren't limited or biased in the products they can offer.

No one provider has a lock on the best products in every category, so you want someone who represents a multitude of companies, who can put together the best financial plan possible and fund it with all the latest and greatest vehicles that are out there.

#5: Education Should Be Ongoing

There are a lot of different designations and certifications for financial professionals. At our firm, we believe the CERTIFIED FINANCIAL PLANNER™ (CFP®) designation to be the core designation in the business today. It has its own code of ethics, and the college-level coursework must be completed before you sit for the certification exam. In addition, CFP® professionals must complete thirty credit hours of continuing education every two years, including two hours of ethics training.

You should know what it takes for a person to achieve the various letters that appear on their business card. Don't be afraid to ask or to research what it took to achieve the designation. Many times, it might simply be paying a fee or taking a weekend course.

#6: Look at Experience and Depth on the Bench

Not only should you look at the credentials after their name, but also the experience that comes with it. Many credentials, such as the CFP®, have an experience requirement. If you like a financial professional but they are close to retirement age, make sure they have an experienced team backing them up as a succession plan. If the advisor is in the twilight of their career, you should know what type of transition plan is in place, should they retire at some point during your retirement.

#7: Do Some Detective work

There are a couple of quick checks you can do to be sure your financial professional is who and what they say they are. With FINRA BrokerCheck, you can check to see if a financial professional or firm is registered to sell securities, offer investment advice, or both. And you can get some information on employment history, licensing, regulatory actions, arbitrations and complaints. You also can do a database search through the SEC Investment Adviser Search. And, if it's appropriate, check your state's office of insurance regulation.

For backup, you might try the Better Business Bureau or just do a Google search. You may find the financial professional declared bankruptcy recently, or that they haven't paid their taxes—and then you can decide if that's really the person you want handling your life savings.

What Does the Financial Planning Process Look Like?

Once you've taken these steps, you can feel pretty good about making the correct choice. Then, it's all about personality, communication, and your general comfort level when you meet.

When you sit down with an advisor, the overall process should look something like our Retirement Roadmap process, as follows:

Step #1: Establishing the Client-Planner Relationship

Often, individuals who come in for an initial visit have learned about our firm either through the radio program that we do, or they've attended one of our workshops, so they know just a little bit about us, and they're interested in knowing more. Establishing the client-planner relationship is our first step.

It is important to make certain that you understand the client-planner relationship. What is your relationship as a client with the financial planner or the retirement planner? What will it look like? How often will you meet? What is the fee structure? What are the expectations? You may also want to find out what type of clients the advisor specializes in working with. At the start, first on the list, is to establish, define, and understand the client-planner relationship.

Next, as we talk about what a relationship with us would look like, we walk you through the Retirement Roadmap Review process. In fact, you don't even have to engage us to have us go through that process with you.

Step #2: Gathering Client Data

Next, the advisor needs to gather your financial data, including your goals for retirement. Gathering data to put your plan together includes two different elements. First is what's called hard data. What are you invested in? What are the details of your pension? When do you plan to retire? What will your social security benefit be? Those are all hard facts.

The other element is learning about your goals, aspirations, and personality—what we call the soft facts. They are just as important as the hard facts. This could be wanting to provide a legacy for your children, knowing you can't tolerate a lot of risk, wanting the peace of mind of knowing income is covered, or wanting to downsize the home at some point in retirement. The second step is critical, and it may require some thinking on your end to figure out what you really want out of retirement.

Step #3: Analyzing & Evaluating the Client's Financial Status

The advisor next needs to analyze and evaluate your current financial status as compared to your goals. Many times, what we see when individuals come into our office is that there is a disconnect between what they say is important and how their money is invested.

Our analysis consists of two main elements. One is a risk analysis of your portfolio, and the other is a retirement income plan.

The biggest disconnect always seems to be the risk level of the portfolio versus the risk tolerance. Most clients are taking more risk than they want, and more risk than they need to.

The income projection is designed specifically for you, and it seeks to answer two main questions: Are you going to be able to meet your expenses with the money that you've saved? What rate of return do you need on your assets, over time, to meet those goals?

We then match the retirement income plan with the risk analysis to find out if you're on the right track and if it is possible that you will be able to reach the goals that you have.

Step #4: Developing recommendations and/or alternatives

If you choose to work with us, we'll begin formulating our recommendations into an easy-to-understand one-page Retirement Roadmap, and proceed with the investment meetings to implement the recommendations.

We believe it is prudent to revisit the plan at least once per year to make sure the recommendations are still in line with each client's individual goals and objectives. It also provides us with an opportunity to find out from our client if any of their goals have changed during the year. For all of these reasons, this final step is as important as those that preceded it.

Our process lines up with the CERTIFIED FINANCIAL

PLANNER™ Board of Standards, and we continue to adhere to those standards by monitoring the relationship over time to make sure that if any changes occur in specific circumstances or goals, we adjust for them. Obviously, you need to inform us when goals change. That way, we are meeting the highest professional standards and doing our utmost for you, our client.

CHAPTER 9

WHEN SHOULD I FILE FOR SOCIAL SECURITY?

"What's right about America is that although we have a mess of problems, we have great capacity - intellect & resources - to do something about them."

— Henry Ford II

Guaranteed sources of income in retirement provide peace of mind and income regardless of what the market is doing, and they continue paying out for as long as you live. The first source of guaranteed income that most retirees are eligible for is social security.

Think of social security as a government-run pension plan. The government had to do the same thing your company did with the pension: save money, invest the money, make assumptions about rates of return and longevity, and pay out for a lifetime. Just like many pension plans, they made some miscalculations along the way. Because of this, there is undoubtably some uncertainty in terms of if/when changes will be made, in the form of benefit cuts, increased taxation, or cost-of-living reductions. However, they aren't offering you any type of buyout, just the monthly payments.

So, your only decision is *when* to file for social security.

Today, Social Security benefits represent on average a third of retirees' income. Nearly 90 percent of Americans sixty-five and older receive some type of Social Security benefit. For many autoworkers, their expenses may be covered by social security and their pension, allowing their other assets to accumulate. But, like the pension decision, it's something that needs to be carefully evaluated and planned out in accordance with the overall retirement income plan. Retirees in the auto world vary significantly from a financial standpoint, so it would be a disservice to make a blanket statement and say taking early or deferring is the right answer.

Your social security benefit amount varies depending on when you apply for benefits; the earliest you can claim is at sixty-two, and the latest you can claim is at seventy. Exceptions can be made to file early for disability and widows. If you claim your benefit prior to reaching your full retirement age (FRA), the SSA reduces your benefit amount by a percentage for each month prior to your full retirement age. For example, if you were born in 1960 and retire at sixty-two (2022), you'll get 70 percent of your monthly benefits. If you retire at sixty-five, you'll get 86.7%.

Full retirement age varies—the full retirement age is sixty-six years and two months for those born in 1955 and gradually increases to sixty-seven for people born in 1960 and later. If a retiree takes benefits prior to their full retirement age, their benefits will be permanently reduced. The full retirement age is when recipients will be able to receive their full benefits (or 100 percent of their calculated benefits). Benefits will increase by 8 percent per year for those who decide to delay collecting Social Security beyond their full retirement age. Recipients who wait until they're seventy to collect benefits will receive 24-percent higher payments (three years of 8-percent increases).

Both choices (retiring early at sixty-two or delaying until the age of seventy) have advantages and disadvantages.

The case for taking social security earlier could be as simple as you like the peace of mind of knowing that social security and your pension cover the bills. Or that you want the money now while you're in your prime retirement years, and you understand there may be some lost dollars on the backend of retirement.

You might not even need the money, but you do not trust the government. You want to get your money out now and invest it yourself for the long haul. That's perfectly fine. You realize that if you take earlier, that's less of a spenddown on your invested assets, and that allows you time to grow these assets for future income, or wealth transfer.

The case for deferring can also be made. You may want to defer as long as possible to maximize the survivor benefit for your spouse.

If you or your spouse lives into your nineties, you are way into the money since you maxed out the benefit.

Or, imagine this, you've retired and taken the lump sum, and since you're not taking social security, your income for the upcoming year is near zero. Well, that would present some interesting tax-planning opportunities, wouldn't it? With zero income, you could spend IRA money at the lowest rates. Or better yet, convert IRA money to Roth IRA at these low rates.

Again, with social security, there is no single solution that's the best in every scenario. We would highly recommend having a social security analysis ran by a financial advisor to see what the optimal strategy would look like in a retirement income analysis.

Pensions and social security provide guaranteed income streams that last as long as you do. This income can act as a foundation to your overall plan—no matter what the market is doing, you will get these monthly deposits into your bank account. If you opt to not take the pension, that guaranteed payment on a monthly basis may only be made up of social security, which is why many retirees look to an annuity to provide another guaranteed source of income to supplement social security.

Just like the pension lump sum decision, the timing on filing for social security is unique to each individual. How is your health? Your spouse's health? If you elected the pension, what is the survivor rate on the pension? If you take the lump sum, are you planning to Roth Convert? Are there assets you can live off with a reasonable withdrawal rate if you let social security defer?

No matter your answers to these questions, it would be wise to have a financial advisor run a social security analysis to show you the potential scenarios and how much each would pay over different life expectancies. Again, there is no one-size-fits-all social security strategy that wins out for everyone—it is a completely personal decision that varies from one client to the next.

When we're building a plan, we plan for our clients to live to a hundred years old. Social security has the potential to payout upwards of $1 million over the remainder of your life, so it's not a decision you want to take lightly, as this could affect your retirement for years to come.

CHAPTER 10

HOW DO ANNUITIES WORK?

> *"If I had asked people what they wanted, they would have said faster horses."*
>
> - Henry Ford

No financial strategy is more polarizing than annuities. Some financial professionals love them. Some hate them. And some claim to hate them—but only certain kinds. This is all extremely confusing for the average investor.

Take Wade Pfau, PhD, CFA and Professor of Retirement Income at the American College of Financial Services. He states that "A fixed-indexed annuity serves as a tool to enhance retirement asset protection by managing market volatility and the sequence of returns risk in the pivotal years leading to retirement. This can better set the stage for retirement and for creating more lifetime retirement income from a given asset base." [11]

Or take Roger Ibbotson, PhD and Professor in the Practice Emeritus of Finance at Yale School of Management. He recently completed a study back-testing equity, fixed income, and fixed index annuity combinations, and concluded the following: "I'm not necessarily advocating you go all in" on fixed indexed annuities, Ibbotson says. "I think combinations of stocks and bonds and fixed indexed annuities are good." [12]

Lastly, how about personal finance expert Suze Orman? If you have ever watched her TV show, many times Suze will be emphatically against annuities, and for good reason. However, she also recognizes that they can have a place in a retirement portfolio. Suze claims that "if you don't want to take risk but still want to play the stock market, a good index annuity might be right for you." [13]

Today's retiree is learning that there is an important place for an annuity when creating a retirement plan. We're of the opinion that annuities can be a wonderful tool if used properly. They also can be a real headache if used improperly, or if you're sold one as a standalone solution rather than as part of an overall financial plan. Our belief is that there are two main use cases for an annuity in a retirement portfolio:

#1: Guaranteed Lifetime Income

For those in need of additional guaranteed income, an annuity can be a great fit for helping protect against living too long. It can also provide a tremendous benefit, in delivering an uncorrelated income stream that isn't dependent on the stock or bond market.

#2: Safe Growth

If you're buying an annuity expecting to match or exceed market returns, you will likely be disappointed. However, it's no secret that a balanced retirement portfolio should consist of both equities and fixed income, with fixed income acting as the stable portion of the portfolio. Since we are now in a rising-interest-rate environment, we can't expect the same returns out of fixed income. Therefore, an annuity may be a viable alternative to provide the safe, stable growth formerly provided by fixed income.

Rich's father used to say, "That's why they make Chevys and Fords," whenever he wanted to explain the differences in people. The fact is, there are at least as many different types of financial vehicles as there are motor vehicles from which to choose, and often this can be overwhelming.

Annuities are not suitable for everyone: It all comes down to personal choice. Your circumstances, income, financial resources, objectives, tolerance for market risk, and investment timeline are all very unique to you. There is no one cookie-cutter investment and/or retirement plan that is a perfect fit for all retirees. That's what makes investing so complex—trying to figure out the best solution to meet your needs.

An annuity is a contract you purchase from an insurance company. For the premium you pay, you receive certain fixed and/or variable growth options able to compound, tax-deferred, until withdrawn. When you are ready to receive income distributions, this vehicle offers a variety of guaranteed payout options through a process known as "annuitization."

Most annuities have provisions that allow you to withdraw a percentage of earnings each year up to a certain limit. However, withdrawals can reduce the value of the death benefit, and excess withdrawals above the restricted limit may incur "surrender charges" within the term of the contract (typically seven to ten years).

Because they are designed as a long-term retirement income vehicle, annuity withdrawals made before age 59.5 are subject to a 10 percent penalty, and withdrawals may be subject to income taxes.

There are four types of annuities:

#1: The Deluxe Model: Variable Annuity

A variable annuity is comprised of professionally managed portfolios that vary in both investment objectives and representative holdings. You may allocate your purchase payments across any number of these portfolios in whatever percentages you choose, with regard for your financial objectives and tolerance for market risk. Taxes on earnings from these portfolios are not due until distributed, and you may transfer assets between portfolios without having to pay taxes on gains.

However, because these various portfolios are managed by professional money managers, the fees you pay for each portfolio, combined with the overall administrative, mortality and expense fees, have the potential to be quite high. Many variable annuities also offer optional riders guaranteeing minimum annual income for a specific number of years or even for life, available for an additional fee. Annuities with optional income riders tend to have fees commensurate with the additional risks as underwritten by the issuing insurer.

#2: Drive off the Lot: Immediate Annuity

With an immediate annuity, you use a lump sum of money to purchase a contract from an insurance company in return for a guaranteed series of payouts. This stream of income is guaranteed for a specified period of time or for the rest of your (and even your spouse's) life—no matter how long you live.

The amount of the payout is based on several factors:
- How much money you use to buy the contract
- The interest rate environment at the time you purchase the contract
- The payout option and timing of your first payment
- Your life expectancy—based on current age and gender
- Any additional features you choose

Immediate annuity income payouts may be either level or increasing periodic payments for a fixed term of years or until the end of your life, whichever is longer. While an immediate annuity can provide reliable income to help cover fixed living expenses, it does not offer substantial potential for growth.

This type of annuity is most similar to your pension, as there is no accumulation phase and you must annuitize immediately to receive income distributions. Once you annuitize with the Life Only option, you forfeit access to your assets. When you die, all of your money that could have been left to your heirs is forfeited to the insurance company (unless you selected an option that continues payments to the beneficiaries).

#3: Safety Rated: Fixed Annuity or Multi-Year Guaranteed Annuity (MYGA)

A fixed annuity provides a guaranteed interest rate for a specific number of years to protect you from market fluctuations. Fixed annuities offer fixed interest rate periods over one, three, five, seven, or ten years, as well as a variety of annuitization payout options—including the option for guaranteed income for life.

The fixed annuity can help you conservatively accumulate assets to help cover fixed living expenses in retirement, but it does not offer substantial potential for growth.

#4: Hybrid: Fixed Indexed Annuity (FIA)

With a fixed indexed annuity, the contract issuer may credit your account value with a guaranteed minimum rate of return on your premium, plus the potential for additional gains linked to the performance of a specific market index—usually the S&P 500. At the end of each contract year, the insurance company measures the growth of the linked index over the previous twelve months and then credits your contract value with that growth, up to a predetermined cap. It may be an annual cap, a monthly cap, or a percentage of the growth of the index.

Because the fixed indexed annuity is linked to an unmanaged index, it tends to have lower administrative fees than a variable annuity. Some fixed indexed annuities allow you to withdraw earnings without penalty up to a certain amount each year. However, be aware that excess withdrawals may incur surrender fees and may also void the credit from the index-linked return.

Typically, the FIA's index-linked interest rate is computed based on one of three methods:

i. **Participation Rate** – If the insurance company sets the participation rate at 60 percent, your fixed indexed annuity will be credited with 60 percent of the return rate experienced by the linked index. So, if the index gained 10 percent, then the annuity would be credited 6%.

ii. **Spread/Margin/Asset Fee** – This is the return rate of the linked index minus a percentage. For example, if the index gained 8 percent and the spread/margin/asset fee is 2 percent, then the annuity would be credited 6 percent.

iii. **Interest Rate Cap** – Some FIAs allow you to benefit fully from index gains up to a specific percentage cap. This is the maximum growth percentage the annuity may earn. If the cap was 5 percent and the index did 8 percent, you would receive the maximum growth of 5 percent.

A fixed indexed annuity is designed to work in any type of market environment. Whether up, down, or flat, the fixed indexed annuity provides downside protection and the potential for gains linked to the performance of a market index.

As long as you abide by the terms of the contract, your principal is guaranteed against market loss from day one, and your interest gains typically lock in each year on your contract anniversary and cannot be taken away in a future market downturn.

For those still confused, let's put it in simple terms for you:

A variable annuity is similar to mutual funds, in that you have various investment options, referred to as "subaccounts." Just like investing in a 401(k), you can choose to be aggressive, moderate, or conservative. Your account value benefits from the upside of the markets, but it also is vulnerable to market losses.

An immediate annuity is similar to a pension, in that it gives you a payment for life (or a selected time period) and has no cash value to pass to your beneficiaries.

A fixed annuity is similar to a certificate of deposit (CD), in that you give an insurance company a lump sum of money, and they offer you a fixed rate of return over the agreed-upon time period (an annuity is not FDIC insured).

A fixed indexed annuity (FIA) or hybrid annuity is similar to fixed income in that it provides a safer, more stable growth rate compared to the at-risk portion of your portfolio.

Annuity Riders can also be added to the above contracts to enhance or tailor the features of the contracts. These riders can vary from providing guaranteed income without the need to annuitize right away, to enhancing the death benefit or adding long-term care features.

CONCLUSION

"I feel pretty good. I never thought I'd live this long. They told me in 1960 that I had less than five years to live."
— Carroll Shelby

As these chapters have defined, you are faced with several life-changing decisions at retirement, which may be some of the most important decisions that you will ever make—with financial and quality-of-life consequences that, quite literally, last a lifetime (or longer!).

1. Do I take the lifetime pension or the lump sum?
2. If I take the lump sum, how can I keep it protected from market volatility while still generating consistent income?
3. What do I do with my 401(k)?
4. How do I find a trusted advisor to help with all of this?
5. When do I take my social security?

Please do your best not to get overwhelmed or anxious. When retirement arrives, you will have an immediate decision to make: monthly payments, or lump sum? That's the first question. It is your pension, and your choice. Your pension is a promise that the company made to you when your employment began, to provide you with money when you retire. Because the company has made you that promise, at some time in the future they are going to have to pay out money to you. That's good news.

Your deciding to take the lump sum has definite advantages for the company, but it's not a trick or a scam. They would rather not have that future liability sitting there on their balance sheet and would rather be done with it. But you need to decide what is best for you and your family. You have options, and they ought to be considered carefully. If you take a monthly payout, the risk is on the company. You receive a steady, predictable stream of income in retirement. On the other hand, if you decide to take a lump sum payment, you have many potential benefits, but you are now responsible for investing the money. In other words, it's on you.

When you are facing this decision, it is important to understand that your pension is guaranteed, up to a certain extent, by the federal government.

As you contemplate how to proceed, carefully evaluating your options is essential to making an informed decision. There are a number of questions worth considering. Among them: Are you responsible with money? How will you invest this money in combination with your 401(k)? How will you generate income from this money in combination with Social Security? How will your decision—lump sum or monthly pension payments—affect loved ones? How can you find an advisor to help with all of this?

As you sit in the hot seat and are forced to answer these potential million-dollar questions, please remember you have us as a lifeline. We can help narrow these options down for you and give you our best and honest advice.

We'll run a Retirement Income Analysis, which will provide you with a better understanding of the impact of each of your choices. There are risks and rewards with both options, whether you opt to take the lump sum or the monthly payments. It is worth carefully considering them in the context of your own individual financial objectives and concerns. This is not a cookie-cutter decision—one size does not fit all. Everyone's individual circumstances differ from those of other family members, or co-workers, or neighbors.

We can't emphasize enough how important it is for you to put this decision in a financial context, specific to your own financial circumstances and objectives. The best way to do that is to have an overall retirement plan, or financial plan. Regardless of what you call it, having such an analysis done, in accordance with best practices adhered to by a CERTIFIED FINANCIAL PLANNER™ professional, can make a significant difference as you weigh the options with retirement just around the corner, and are faced with the pension decision of your life.

Thank you for picking up this book and taking the time to read through it. Hopefully, it has been very helpful for you, as you look ahead to the not-too-distant future when you will be faced with these all-important decisions.

We've tried to present the material in an easy-to-understand way, one that will provide you with an effective framework to move through your decision-making process, suggesting ways for you to evaluate your choices, understand your options, and make the best possible decision for you and your family. As we've mentioned, this is your decision. Every circumstance—financial and otherwise—is different. But there are steps you can take, as we've attempted to lay out clearly and concisely, that can provide the facts you need to make an informed decision.

Knowing the critical questions that need to be asked, being aware of the data and analysis that can inform your decision, and understanding that it's worth the time, effort and energy to proceed along the steps we've outlined can help to give you the confidence you need to make your decision.

We have helped a great many clients at Richard W. Paul & Associates respond to these critical financial decisions regarding their retirement. For many people, they have been trying to accumulate as much money as possible and have not considered these crucial retirement decisions at all, during their career and working years. All of a sudden, it seems, they need to make decisions. Our firm has extensive experience working with retirees—and soon-to-be retirees—in a wide range of circumstances, and much of the wisdom that we offer comes from understanding what other retirees have gone through as they enter their retirement years.

As the saying goes, knowledge is power. And through our experience and professional expertise, we seek to empower you—and work with you, every step of the way. The importance of these decisions can't be overestimated. What you decide will have ramifications for your financial security and your quality of life. But you absolutely can make a wise decision—one that is best for you.

Again, thank you for spending time with this book, and the information that has been shared. Please keep in mind the steps that have been outlined here, and don't hesitate to turn to us for help. That's why we're here.

Lastly, congratulations again, and cheers to a successful retirement!

If there is anyone you know who you think would find this book helpful, please have them visit

www.BigThreeRetiree.com

to request a copy.

SOURCES

[1] "Weighted Average Interest Rate Table." *Internal Revenue Service*, www.irs.gov/retirement-plans/weighted-average-interest-rate-table.

[2] PGIM, Inc. *Longevity and Liabilities: Bridging the Gap.* 2 Nov. 2018, www.pgim.com/pgimdoc/getsecuredoc?file=2495471F79FD34A485258339004481A3.

[3] Society of Actuaries Mortality Improvement Scale, MP-2017 https://www.soa.org/experience-studies/2017/mortalityimprovement-scale-mp-2017/ (Jun. 2018)

[4] Wynne, Trilbe. "Defined Benefit Funding Rises Even as Returns Turn Negative." *Pensions & Investments Online*, 29 April 2019, https://tinyurl.com/y4ns9evc.

[5] Burr, Barry B. "Mixed Opinions on GM's Plan to Transfer $29 Billion to Prudential." *Pensions & Investments*, 22 Aug. 2012, https://tinyurl.com/y4dprf5w.

[6] Braham, Lewis. "The Stretch IRA Is About To Snap Under the Secure Act." *Barron's*, 6 July 2019, www.barrons.com/articles/the-stretch-ira-is-about-to-snap-under-the-secure-act-51562414402.

[7] Jackson, Tony. "GM Shows Gravity of Pension Challenge." *Financial Times*, 7 June 2009, https://tinyurl.com/y3ngu755.

[8] Ferretti, Christine. "Detroit Bankruptcy 'Threw Everything into Chaos' for Retirees." *Detroit News*, The Detroit News, 19 July 2018, www.detroitnews.com/story/news/local/detroit-city/2018/07/18/detroit-bankruptcy-retirees-reaction/783828002/.

[9] "Quantitative Analysis of Investor Behavior, 2019," DALBAR, Inc. www.dalbar.com

[10] "Cost of Long Term Care by State: 2018 Cost of Care Report." *Genworth*, www.genworth.com/aging-and-you/finances/cost-of-care.html.

[11] Pfau, Wade. *MANAGING RISK WITH FIXED-INDEXED ANNUITIES*. June 2018, greatamericanria.com/docs/librariesprovider2/agent-document-library/ria/managing-risk-with-fixed-indexed-annuities-in-the-pre-retirement-years.pdf.

[12] Ibbotson, Roger G. *Fixed Indexed Annuities: Consider the Alternative*. Zebra Capital Management, LLC, Jan. 2018.

[13] Orman, Suze. *The Road to Wealth*. Riverhead Books, 2001.

Made in the USA
Monee, IL
05 February 2020